VIA Folios 105

A WOMAN UNKNOWN IN HER BONES

Poems by Rachel Guido deVries

Library of Congress Control Number: 2014944620.

COVER ART: Pat Byrne
www.artonapage.com

© 2014 by Rachel Guido deVries

All rights reserved. Parts of this book may be reprinted only by written permission from the author, and may not be reproduced for publication in book, magazine, or electronic media of any kind, except for purposes of literary reviews by critics.

Printed in the United States.

Published by
BORDIGHERA PRESS
John D. Calandra Italian American Institute
25 West 43rd Street, 17th Floor
New York, NY 10036

VIA FOLIOS 105
ISBN 978-1-59954-069-6

for Jerry Berrigan

Some of these poems have appeared in *Paterson Literary Review, The Syracuse Cultural Workers' Women's Date Book, 2010, Sojourners Magazine, Voices in Italian Americana,* and *Stone Canoe.*

Contents

Unknown in Her Bones	7
Peaches	8
Circle	9
Black Birds Sing	10
Reindeer in My Mother's Eyes	11
Parakeet	12
Death Gift	13
When I Die	14
Winter Morning	15
Imperfection	16
Practice	17
The Foot Doctor Dreams of Herkimer	18
Now and Then and Now	19
Went Weeping, Little Bones, But Where	20
Ice	22
Knives	23
Poet's Lament	24
Mornings	25
Perhaps	26
Holy Thursday	27
Saint Cat	28
Oh, Let Me Dream	29
Tears	30
Somewhere in Deep Sky	31
Wing	32
Oh, We've All Forgotten	33
Playing School	35
Coal	36
Stone	37
My Father's Hands	38

I Dream of Fig Trees	39
I Am	40
Life Stories	41
Holy Rest	42
Gratitude	43
Love	44
Purple Portrait of a Stranger at Long Nook	45
Love Poem After a Quarrel	46
Just Before	47
Geography Lesson	48
Everyday Faith	49
Marriage	50
Beginning of a Kiss	51
Listen	52
Solitude	53
At the Hermitage	54
Like Writing a Story of Bliss	55
Question	56
Sound and Sound Again	57
Once a Praying Mantis	58
Praying with Trees	59
Underneath Bones	60
Lost Love Song	61
Oh, Great Peach	62
First, Take Two	63
Light	64
After the Wedding	65
Old Bird, Young Song	66
Wild	67

Unknown in Her Bones

Everywhere I look there's a woman unknown,
unknown in her bones, in her skin, in the way
her dreams sharpen and thin. The last years hover,
they glint like bright snow, they tease and lament
and laugh fully.

I am a woman unknown in her bones, unknown
to her bones: This fleshy marvel of my years,
this autumn day and time, this mind that roams
and pauses and broods some days on all my losses.
A small fall wind, its scent still flutters
 in any woman all full of bones,
the beginning of love unknown.

PEACHES
                  (after Mom, October 15, 1923-July 17, 2006)

Eating peaches with my mother
in the garden of her love,
when hope bloomed
like Jersey peaches.
We ate, soft whispers of peach skin
sliding from the peach, sweet
juice shiny on our chins. A peach
in a dish late summer.

My lover runs a bath. Love waits.
Death is behind us for now, yet
lurks along the edges of life. Ah, life,
as short as the season of peaches, as sweet.

CIRCLE

who mothered the pearls when rain came washing away
her tears. Tears are like pearls, my mother always said, fingering
the pearls he gave her long after the clouds had lifted, long
after the lonely nights were strung like pearls of tears
around her throat, long after the language of birds had gone,
and his songs swayed the horizon throaty and blue

who mothered the pearls, oysterless, their sandy beds bereft,
their shells squandered along rocky shoals where sorry
stopped. It was me, rising up in a night when the moon
shone like a pearl, opalescent and fat as a woman's belly
where an oyster had been and where now a pearl nestled,
an infant in my mother's hands

Black Birds Sing

Two black birds share a branch and sing,
sing to the raindrops fat and blue dancing
among trees. Way down underneath
a dark-eyed fish swims through sea air,
opens its mouth, catches the rain,
swims in songs of black birds.
In the vanishing rain four memories
wash the window. Home. The baby.
Two lovers. The rest blows into the trees
where black birds sing, or used to.

Reindeer in My Mother's Eyes

The deer came today, Mamma, hours after
grieving you again over coffee, solitary at 4 a.m.,
missing your voice, your hand on my cheek.

You loved the deer, reindeer you called them,
a child's view, you at 80, full of wonder,
your New Jersey self awed by the magic
of deer in my back yard.

Today neighbors throw out bread.
Round slices spin to the deer, six of them,
mothers and babies. They bow their heads to earth,
lift the bread like Eucharist to their mouths.

The last time I saw you, Mamma, I gave you
communion, a small circle of bread, the body
of hope as yours was failing. You closed your eyes
like a child of eight, and lifted your tongue
to be nourished and sweetened by love.

Years ago, we delighted in windfall apples
we made into pies. The apple tree is gone now.
The old tire swing is gone too. So are you,
Mamma, irretrievable yet beside me now,
arriving with the deer, gracing the yard.

PARAKEET

>   *for Katie*

When she lost her parakeet
everything came loose, feathers
flying skyward, yellow and blue.
His sharp little beak stayed quiet.
His eyes though, two black tiny beads,
met hers at the last and held, for a moment,
all her love.

This is why she cries now, guitar
slung over a shoulder. Its strummed
notes don't match the beauty of her little
bird's song or his small vulnerable body.
She stroked and stroked the softness
she knew was dying, was flying
right out of her teenage hands.

Death Gift

They hang the clothes all cockeyed on the line
in the big backyard, so she enjoys
disorder, watches colors mix and dance with wind,
drift beyond clouds into hills turning red.
Her blood thins. She grows dizzy with pleasure.
All the mysteries of her faith were solved.

It's like that at the end of movies, too—
the moment colors shift, dance, settle.
Her sisters know she needs some wildness
before she sinks into pillows, sighs,
turns her withered face toward the window
where riotous clothes collide and sleep comes
full of life.

When I Die

No one will remember that I could be silly
and talked out loud in the lonely kitchen
No one will remember that I cooked great meals
or made people laugh or cry or
scream in rage

     this is liberating and invites me
to look at hope and eternity, magical thinking
that keeps us here, rooted to earth, tilting at times
toward the lure of ownership. Then back
through the labyrinth to calm, which I name faith. It's
like an echo of a bible story: when I call out loud or grab
the hem of my fleet savior I am me again, the answer
is light—sun unlocking clouds rosy
inside my chest

            I dance, hold lovely arms
perfume, pleasure, and peace. I arrive
where I imagine:. Heart up,
Hands open, singing in this body of life.

WINTER MORNING

        Late morning in winter invites
writing in bed, silent, snowy.
I meditate on noise, busy world,
voices, until they fade,
almost vanish

        to birds singing:
thin-bellied blue tones, silence

                a river sounding
all the way to the thrill in my belly,
now suffused by blue waves.
Birds sing true as any prophet's words, echoes
through hills, time, the poem's voice
still, in my hands.

IMPERFECTION

Imperfection is the place where the spirit enters,
the small hole in your shirt, the loosening threads
of carpet, an ache for forgiveness.
Where the camel waits, the eye strays,
the hand reaches up, empty of all but breath,
is the place where the soul begins, its gravity mightier
than we may know. There, where the rug unravels
like a rope of time, pockets bleed their secrets
between the seams. In a widow's eyes words appear
lit up like stars in a deep sky: If God is all we believe,
sorrow and bliss, the soul is breath, stone and lattice,
ligature and air. It lives in the body's secret lapses.
How grateful then to know imperfection's door swinging
open and closed, how good to be humbled.

PRACTICE

Seeing the holy in everyday life
is spiritual practice. War wounds
blossom like tulips in snow,
exploding bombs are gods' trombones.
Get down on your knees
and open to the ear of a soldier, breathe
fire into it, whisper Beatitudes and hope
somehow it matters. You might offer
the small white wings of a butterfly
to one in despair, a poet's hope
perched inside the soul. Better yet,
make a plate of sandwiches to nourish
the hungry. Your life is gospel,
prayers and love. Measure your footsteps.
You step into the beautiful grass
and it welcomes you every time, spirit to spirit,
just like small birds chirping and darting
that you love to look at. Listen, they sing
every day, and every day you have a choice
to open your mouth and full-throated sing
your song. Sing the spirit to life.
Let it enter the sky. Let it speak.
Let it practice. Let it be holy.

The Foot Doctor Dreams of Herkimer

She's afraid to fly, my foot doctor, worrying
about her flight to Jamaica. She's not dreaming
of sunshine and beaches. Watching the snow blow,
she'd rather go to Herkimer, a place she knows.
She is afraid to fly. Of course she is.

She knows what can happen when feet leave
the ground and the body for a moment
touches heaven. She doesn't want to be loose,
to float forever the way a spaceman might,
released from ties and unfamiliar sky.

Feet come attached to person and to earth,
their problems can be met and often fixed.
They can walk, if they need to, all the way
to Herkimer and back, never asking why or how,
and never needing or wanting to ever leave the ground.

Now and Then and Now

I love my body, breaking down as it does,
fragile with life. From windows of bone,
spirits of children kept home
begin to roam free: the wide-eyed wondering one,
the one hurt by someone's leaving, the jealous child
I still must be. The tender one, stroking the soft,
broken wing of a bird I buried near the lilac tree.
I prayed over purple blossoms for a peaceful life.

My knees bent easily. Prayers chimed like
shiny coins, round as the Eucharist each Sunday,
the body made sweeter with its kiss.

In silence prayers emerge as poems, poems
as prayers. Poet, penitent, I praise the body.
Its bones soften like bread, and now and then
like something holy.

WENT WEEPING, LITTLE BONES, BUT WHERE?
       (from "I Cry, Love! Love!"
       by Theodore Roethke, Collected Poems)

      1

And oops I went, sorrowful again, weeping
for my little bones that splinter in my sleep.
Awake, knees and tendons snap and crack
and here I am upside down again. It's
the dog's fault, pulling on the leash
the way she does, hungry for ice and snow
or a juicy bone, while mine dry up,
kindling for a fire.

      2

The four cats come close, flicking their sensuous
tails at one another, rubbing first on me, then blanket
and pillow and breath. One nuzzles beneath my chin,
another approaches my shoulder and cries. They cheer
me up against the glass where the sun is rising. Snow
slides off the rooftop, piles up on the deck.

      3

Lover sleeps late and I hobble to the kitchen,
my thumping cane and my terror-moves

recall my father at the end, when every step
was a danger. His shoulders hunkered down
like little soldiers, waiting to shoot or be shot.
I aim my cane at the window, drag the newspaper
home through the chute and wait for the coffee
to brew. The blue sky worries me. Life. Beauty.
Fear.

4

Later, friends will surround the table.
Sauce, stuffed shells and the hobbled poet.
They with their ennui and their charm,
their love and their convention. Oh!
I envy them so. I will laugh and light
candles while my bones smolder, turn to ash.
I weep for them. Wasps
buzz close, pigeons fly away. This
is the beginning of life
as shaky as my knees,
unsteady on all the ice.

ICE

Ice shifts and cracks beneath my feet,
tries to bring me down, slide me,
break bones or heart.

Sinister and lovely.
Threatens and glistens. If
I fall, if I give into falling,

sliding on ice whose purpose it is
to pull me off balance, ice
calling out in shiny voices,
from small glittering throats.

I am jealous of what is there,
what I do not know about
how it works

              ice
beneath the surface
silvery blue water stuns and beckons

KNIVES

Knives dense as thieves land to er
and clash, metal against metal, to like.
Their slender sheathes menace spoons
nestled into each others' slopes valleys.
Even the forks, shiny tines pokiopeward,
have a less dangerous aura.

But the knives. Shrill, scraping;p.
an insistent voice telling you ovd over
to cut out your own heart or stmeone else's
and then gang up like thieves, he knives,
skinny as shadows at dusk.

A Woman Unknown — 23el Guido deVries

POET'S LAMENT

A poem
I wrote
has vanished from the

along with any memory
I have of it
what it was about
and I wonder
since I don't

remember it
why
I miss
 it
 so

Mornings

I do not quite recognize the me standing
in the aisle, about to take communion
in the old Catholic church in the city

It's enough too to receive this fire, lovely
with logs I burn. Their spirits
become mountain air. What scent of love

or sorrow still within fills up the sky.
I chant a prayer into morning flames,
fire after rain, my satisfied trees.

A sacred silence falls onto the woods
after rain. Birdsong and breezes sway oak
and aspen. Even the loons stop wailing

from the lake, stunned, I imagine, as I am,
by how it all seems holy.

Perhaps

> "It is fatal to woo yourself
> However graceful the posture."
> —Theodore Roethke

But how else some days to awaken soul
and sinew, embrace myself as well as
the elusive faith that calls home the poem.
Prayer comes naturally by the fire,
ready to welcome desire, faith
erotic as flames of candles in church.
Gratitude lights up my chest. My heart beats.
My spirit is substantial, more like a log
than wispy smoke exhaled or ashes
left behind. It is powerful,
travelling like a river night and day.
What it notices becomes me. I woo
myself like that. I am sometimes graceful,
often headstrong, clumsy, pulling
things after me on my way. Grace
may come in solitude: mornings like this,
when I sit before the fire, head bowed,
and praise the poem, and the gods
inside it all.

HOLY THURSDAY

The first time I washed someone's feet
I marveled at her delicate toes,
her lovely arch, how the ankle supposed
fine bones. I loved the intimate touching
of a place till then unknown to me. On
my knees I praised small things: my love of love,
the God before me, the humble foot
I was given to touch on my way home.

Saint Cat

When the red cat climbs up the trestle of love
to nestle into my sweatshirt, trembling begins,
light as his head on my chest. Early
green trees tumble with memories,
a movie playing in the window. Thunder
rumbles, but it's a ways off, so we'll
wait awhile for drums of rain, zigzag
cracks of lightning, its beautiful fire.

The red cat purrs his holiness,
and makes of himself a circle, rests
for awhile, then wakes and gallops
to the door to go out and ramble toward bliss—
a chipmunk or field mouse, catnip
in the garden, or just to lay in a slant of sunlight,
lolling on grass still sparkling with dew.
Look, he seems to say, how easy it is
to be grateful.

Oh, Let Me Dream

Oh, let me dream about the red stripes of our flag
waving for freedom, soaking up the blood
of war, taming the red spot of rage
in my father's eye, the red of a target drawing
a fiery gun.

Oh, let me dream instead about your lips,
cherry red like Mamma's lipstick,
the red hot flash of love, the taste
spicy as new sex

Oh, come on. The fires of rage and greed
have had their turn, have burned for too
many years. Can't we finally curl up
around the fire, blow a little on the last
sparks, watch the flames blazing,
warm up our lonely blood red hearts.

Tears

Tears fall like seeds into streams.
Trees that grow are trees of sorrow,
kneeling in streams of blue water.

If hope is Aristotle's waking dream,
what faith is yet unseen and believed.
The knocking in my chest is a gate

swinging back and forth in wind and rain,
opening to a dream of trees,
fruit and wisdom their branches.

I try to breathe in
flower, mountain, cloud, star, wind:
Sacred spirit. We are watering the earth

with our losses. Tears spilled out
are best saved for cleansing wounds,
for feeding faith, dreams, those trees.

Somewhere in Deep Sky

for Johnny

It doesn't matter that you're not here,
or that your big bearded face
isn't laughing. I can hear your
footsteps shuffling off to Paradise,
the way you'd imagine it alone,
the way I try to imagine you now:
dancing somewhere in deep sky,
light on your feet, still alive.

WING

A woman named *Wing* crashed her plane in the middle
of no place I'd stop and visit, linger awhile
in moonlight, listen to dry corn stalks whisper
under winter sky.

How perfect a name she had for hope: *Wing*. So
she flew, lighting last in a field of nothing much.
In the wreckage, a landing wheel sticks up
a flag after battle. Wings all burned to ash.

I find relief and sadness in this story.
Naming the end of hope can be soothing.
Sometimes, though, it's just a deserted field,
wing almost a memory.

OH, WE'VE ALL FORGOTTEN

Oh, we've all forgotten, forgotten our names,
our fathers' and grandfathers' names, names
of our mothers, our grandmothers, the buried
boy twins, lost sisters, the one who always
wanted to be white.

Who are we after all? Music from shadows,
arias so old, sung so long. Carved steps
leading home or away from home and back,
back to the clicking of heels on blue tile,
the blue wrapping up of our days.

Remember, he used to say, conspiratorial and wise,
remember.   Remember the O, wide open
mouth full of whys, and the onion, polished
and round, just waiting to enter the dish.
Ah, life. All petri and venom, all heaven and hill.

Remember large plump breasts—somebody's
dream: a shelf to ledge one's
life against. How warm it felt to lie with love,
legs, arms wrapped around ideas. A young man
playing with a matchbook, a car rounding a corner.

What might have happened?
A child. A privileged life, a predictable splitting of seams.

Lost one night in a tent forlorn. Deep in the desert of a love.
All along, I trusted him. Him. Word seldom used now,
once I loved.

I know how the clink of a glass calls us to tables
full of memories, to altars of penance and blessing.
Shhh. They might hear us. All of us who've forgotten
ourselves and our names, our fathers' names,
Gianni, Giuseppe, Salvatore, our mother's names,

Marietta. Raquela, Maria.
The name I call my own bones now: woman.
From them all.

Playing School

When we were little
my sister and I played school
with our crayons in their big tin.
Small, well-used crayons—
reds, yellows, blacks, blues,
became kindergartners. Taller
crayons skipped one-legged
into higher grades, and teachers,
the least used colors, dressed
in straight skirts of burnt sienna
and plain gray, their noses
chartreuse and pointy.

We passed hours at the kitchen table.
In the parlor, Mamma smoked
alone, waiting for love to come home.
Mornings, sister's hand in mine,
we left her and walked to Catholic school,
crayons put away, bright colors mixed in
with colors dull as her gray morning sky.

Coal

Sometimes there was not enough,
so Mamma would light the oven.
We'd sit before it, our campfire,
me Rita, Johnny and Mamma,
eating minute rice with butter
for breakfast.

The he-man of the family was gone, again,
leaving us cold, but happier. How safe it was
before our open oven door, our small circle
of love. Mamma told us stories before school,
then off we'd march, warm and full, to nuns
and classrooms.

She must have been cold, waiting for us
to troop back home. She might look at me, then
grin. "The coal's in ," she'd say,
and we'd know he was back.
"Go throw some in the furnace."

One piece at a time, I tossed that coal
into the red hot fire, imagining.

STONE

Stone. A father's alias, curled in his fists
the name he could not own. Smooth as a stone too,
swaggering into clubhouses of danger. Decades later
I am full of his shame and rage, they rumble
in my little girl's heart. I keep her tucked between my breasts,

her black hair, eyes shut behind secrets,
trapped in a cave of sorrow. An echo
sways sometimes through slits in gray walls,
the key blue as ocean waves humming and it is this
she learns all her life to listen for, a sound,

shimmering on stone in her open palm.

My Father's Hands

My father never had gentle hands
until the end. His hands gave out
the way his mind did, one ability
at a time, one memory at a time,
one hurtful gesture at a time,
until all that was left were his poor hands,
soft now, empty, and so much smaller
than I recalled. He would take those
hands and touch my cheeks, "bella figlia,"
he'd say, at last.

I DREAM OF FIG TREES

I dream of fig trees in the yards
of Sicilian dreamers, uncles,
war veterans, ushers at church,

now gone. Fig trees and gardens
gone from northern backyards
where strangers live

Trembling underground, old bones
of trees rattle memories,
cells of hands that grew them.

I Am

I am the loud mouth balancing
on the blade of your knife
my tongue thick with truths
I've held beneath it
waiting for blood to pour
like rain down the ladder
of my anger, each rung
a memory blue as a bruise.

I am the loud mouth full of power
crackling with my stories and my rage.
This is my element, fire blazing
across the sky on an August night,
years after the air was charged with danger
and no map showed the way back home.

I am the loud mouth
my mouth open in a perfect circle,
brassy and round. I howl my name
and my mother's name and all my sisters'
names. I shout them into the sky, right into
the throat of time, into canyons and oceans
and stars.

LIFE STORIES

Down the road into life, deep into mysteries,
into the smaller bliss of love,
faith, home, and losses. Blessed with this,
I sometimes picture others walking on these floors,
and wonder then where I will be,
or who, or how my fragile life
will one day simply sigh.

  Mamma sighed, a week before she died.
"I never thought it would be like this. I never
thought I'd know the way I'd die."

*Run away from fear, from the beggar cold
on the roadside.* I came to surrender then,
my heart knocking like a long lost relation's.
The voice was the voice of an old friend
who never betrayed. I, the beggar, am coming
in from the cold, unknown, unafraid.

HOLY REST

> *The Rowing Endeth*
> —Anne Sexton

1

I can rest a little here, moored at the dock of love.
"The rowing endeth," the poet called
and deep into the middle of life, I begin
to believe. Lucky in love is a woman I know
who lately has been blessed.

2

Laughter is one of God's gifts. How joy
pleases him and the children we gather,
the humble ones we recognize as kin.
Sharing soup and celebrations we laugh
and sing and pray, the teenage boy's voice
leading us in tonight's sweet prayer. "I have
tears in my eyes," he tells me later. "Someone
I love has just this morning died."

3

A poem is a circle shaped into Eucharist.
Or the Eucharist is love turned into this poem
Either way is lovely, like the end of struggle,
like the beginning of love, like resting
in the hand of the holy.

GRATITUDE

So many women have grown me,
from Mary to Mamma to the loves
of my heart, to prophets and poets
who move me to life. "I can't do this
alone," I once cried out loud, alone
with a habit of grief and smoke. Right
then I was called into faith. So many
prayers have followed, conversations
with those I believe.

"Return again, Return again,
Return to the land of your soul...."

The Rabbi shared this song with us
last night. We lifted our voices, shy
at first, and then together: "Born
and reborn and re..."

awakened, we begin to sing from
the land of our homesick souls.

LOVE

If I grab onto the last branch
and hold on, will I begin
to breathe in the mystery
that lies in nature, in your hands?
I'd swallow sky and devour trees,
let my ears fill with birdsong,
the roar and whisper of fire.
The wind would be me,
spirited by the hope of grace.
Holding on, then letting go of the branch
and the tree it springs from,
filled with it, and singing

Purple Portrait of a Stranger at Long Nook

I love her purples against the sea,
the sweet violet of her as she bends
for shell and stone, the erotic purple
of her soft skirt raised up by purple wind,
the sea behind her dark as a purpled bruise
at the wave's crest, the soft pink of her naked feet
against rain-tanned sand, the purple silence
between each wave where I see her,
violet sweet, bending at the waist,
lovely.

Love Poem After a Quarrel

When hunger appears
on a Sunday afternoon, rain
falling softly in July, I lay
my mouth to yours, wonder how love
comes to be after quarrels, why
we argue as though we despise our lives
and as hours pass we reconcile
without cruel words to mark the air.
Touch again recalls what's there,
besides the mysteries, beneath the fire,
alongside our desire.

Just Before

I ran my hands over the place
where last your right breast rested,
felt its warmth tremble in my palms,
said so long to one piece of you
I loved, that had nestled like a pearl
in our bed, white sheets tumbled, well
slept in. Just before we left
for the hospital you asked me
to kiss the place between your breasts,
a place, you said, you always loved,
a delicate rivulet of skin caressed
on both sides that day. I kissed
and lay my head there. It was
time to go. We said good-bye.
We said hello.

GEOGRAPHY LESSON

              where
a lovely hill filled the vista
there's now a plateau with a river bed.
Once a river ran full. Its furrows
recall fullness. I travel the path
a new way, my hands exploring,
my tongue and lips as well. How
lovely you become this place.
How you are there, still
in the echo of hills.

Everyday Faith

It would seem the cat is oblivious
to death, or the fear death means.
She sits in the windowsill, a late
summer day. We've come home
with two weeks worth of groceries.
Cancer free, the doctor said, his neat
white quiet head tucking down, gentle,
sincere. You found a surgeon much like you.
Quiet. Intense as the scalpel in his hand, the faith
in yours. Gentle. Sincere. And so afraid,
or is it me who fears, or all of our fears,
except for the faithful cat who washes her paws
in afternoon light. We stretch out on our bed near the window
for an afternoon which has an everyday feeling
we begin to practice.

Marriage

Winter again, and geese are flying home.
We look up to sky, see what is unknown.,
calling, scary as death and life.
Here we are, snow on the ground, falling.
We've known doubt. Nearing advent,
it tempts us out. I praise the lulls and hills
of what we dare. Someone in blue walks by,
swathed in trees and gray afternoon light
upon the snow. Whose shadow loped across
the window, the shadowy deer I supposed
on the long road home one night last week
when love had come undone
beneath echoes of beautiful geese.

It is you I see, sylph and soul-full,
the blue that I've pursued in you.
When love returns, as it does
 if love is what is sought, it returns
like the geese, unaware of how they've come
to trust the holy and steady blue sky.

BEGINNING OF A KISS

A kiss not yet kissed, lips never roamed,
tongue, conspirator, stays still

    but the kiss has begun

it thrums through the blood
hovers above dreams
aroused by touch of anything else:
furry kitten purring in her arms,
lip of wine glass, its peachy glow,
robust scent of basil
in her hands

        in everything she knows, all she senses,
the kiss trembles, begins

Listen

Listen baby I love it when your lipstick
marks the glass, I love it when I touch
my lips to yours, wine sweet inside the mouth
like a tongue of love. Who fills the chalice?
I know it's you, sticky sweet lips red
as first blood, holy, made by you. So each time
I touch the glass, the lips, the kiss, the blood,
I'm just a little closer to heaven.

Solitude

Solitude is a mystery, like breath.
Its whispers kiss tender places,
the hurts of being alive.

Free here, I wander under once dreamed trees,
remembering

Skipping stones one summer day
I slipped into a blue stream
and learned solitude's pocket.
I tucked my secrets in.
Like shiny stones, they cheered me,
became poems.

My breath opens, spirited,
the way solitude does, quietly,
its mystery the last window I will look through.

At The Hermitage

Here I am among kin:
bullfrog heron blue bird and bee
deer and coyote and squirrel.
Bunnies cavort and small dogs bark.
The feral cat, the horses neighing
in the near-by field. Chirrups
of cicada grasshopper cricket
and two sisters' laughter early morning.
Coffee and prayer, solitude, call,
this pond still and burbling.

When I wait for the poem, empty as a vessel
before the wine, I am most the poem. Open.
Expectant. Waiting to speak, or more,
waiting, emptied, so I might hear voices

in the birdsong, the bullfrog, the silent step
of deer. Here is my hope, my fear, my words.
In my breath, in my step, in my hungry
hungry heart, I grow still, listen.

Like Writing a Story of Bliss

(After St. John of the Cross)

Prayerful time is like writing a story of bliss.
First solitude, the beautiful trinity:

Body, mind, and soul. Together,
trees and threes offer bliss:
Father-Mother/Daughter-Son/Holy-HolySpirit/

Up here on the tree-filled hill, we believe in mystics.
Deer lope everywhere, untroubled. There is so much
silence,

God might speak of and to all ways,
to labyrinth or pond or tree-tops,

to love songs of the body: an exhilarated foot
set free in the grass, an ear open to seagull or sparrow,

their wings a way into Faith. For a moment
the mind might enter the bliss of the body's

prayer, into the air of the pure soul, its dark night,
welcoming and grateful.

Question

I pose a question out loud.
In response, the whole pond
goes wild, every frog croaking.
I laugh out loud.

Love is a chorus of frogs, every
honored sparrow, each tree and reed
ripple of pond, cloud, heartache
and joy.

Sound and Sound Again

Brown frog-ripples of sound
moving out/the sound/

A bit of wind
Tall grasses sway
and weave
Waving east
Sun just up
Grasses shimmer
Chirp and song
Whistle and caw
The far away dog
Just listen

Once a Praying Mantis

When my mother's face appeared in the dream
It was upturned, smiling, lifting to sun:
a flower, laughing little bells, like belled
petals on lilies of the valley she loved

                        Once
a praying mantis roamed the side garden. I was ten.
I cupped her in my hands, her long and slender body
green, trembling, sacred. Silence
around us as I knelt to the place she dwells

wherever she is—dream, garden, sky,
or in this memory about being alive.

Praying with Trees

This morning I prayed with trees.
Oh! Their leaves clapped together
in ecstasies I'd never known,
They showed me their language of rain and wind, sun
in their branches, roots deep
in earth.

I prayed like the leaves,
my hands together and
reaching high,
trees after welcoming rain
full of praise.

Underneath Bones

Underneath, in the place only the body knows,
stories, simple as bone, wait.
Whole histories stand on white bones
and memories. Love, grief, loss, fortune: still alive,
ulna lonesome as a femur found apart from the patella,
which sounds like a dance, and the funny bone giggles
alongside the forearm, the radius glowing at the notion,
leg and arm and humor. The once bereft
body turns, laughs at its own predictability.
Genes and mothers, bones and common blood sigh, settle in.

Lost Love Song

Lost love songs, small deaths. Giving up is not easy
when pleasure lies there, in between straits
and rivers, changing landscapes of bodies.
Furry moss softens stone. I eat my sorrow,
swallowing hard, make room for blue notes
that may sing like the birds this summer.

Oh Great Peach

She keeps hoping for a soft peachy glow,
a cinematic gesture: the repentant lover
banging on her door at 3 a.m., pleading forgiveness,
full of desire. But when was the last time
her black dress floated upward from the forest floor,
or her dancing lover dipped her low, so her breasts flowed
up, just over lace and buttons, astonished by the gravity of
love.

Oh, great peach, warm with sunlight,
repeal this ban on love,
pit and pity, and bloom by summer,
romantic as a Caribbean post card,
a pair of shoes we shared.

First, Take Two

Maybe we're not starting again,
but you left your toothbrush here,
cozying up to mine in the crystal glass,
and it was good to make love, familiar
as always, though a half year has passed
since you left.

I've rearranged the bed so love could be
new, two of us tumbling in sage green sheets,
though I didn't expect it to be you,
fifteen years ago, or now, and here we are,
again, the first time.

LIGHT

A single firefly lit the room,
flitting from screen to window.
We fluttered the sheets
and found each other in the otherwise
darkness. What is familiar shines now
beneath a new moon, sheer softness, breast,
lithe thighs

          The firefly's flight
is brief. With its double wings, it seeks
only to dine, loving as I do sweet nectar,
to mate, and then find home.

After the Wedding

A voice I call God's came hurtling down from dark skies,
big words were thrown at me: *Love. Trust. Faith.*
I heard you breathing in my red pajamas We are home
pulling stars from a night we believe in.

We cup our hands, like bowls of love. The stars
flutter and dance from my hands to yours, from your hands
to mine. Either way, their light shares our hands,
and each becomes the other.

OLD BIRD, YOUNG SONG

The old bird sings the blues from my throat,
craning her neck against the cell that holds her in.

Let the old bird sing her truth at last, I think.
She plays and flutters her songs.

My tongue tunes up on old saws,
someone's five o'clock shadow sandy on my cheek.

But that was decades ago,
when I was another kind of bird.

I stood with a shovel over my shoulder
and kept on digging, digging, digging,

the sun fiery behind me. It was a long time
before I could kiss my own shadow,

welcome her into the circle of my life.
It was the bird singing in the cell of my throat,

knocking her little beak against my neck 'til I listened.
I cupped her once in the palm of my hand

and felt our tender bodies curve like the notes
of a song. The first note. The beginning.

WILD

> ...wild is anything/beyond the reach of
> purpose not its own.
> —Wendell Berry

The wild heart is a star that yearns to sing
light and voice among endless sky.
Its pulse is river, sea, pine tree
and bird, freedom that sparks up the dark
with song. Voices rise, wildly in love
with the unknowable world.

About the Author

RACHEL GUIDO DEVRIES's last book of poems is *The Brother Inside Me* (Guernica, 2008). Her second children's book is *Stati zitta, Josie!* (Bordighera, 2014). Her first children's picture book, *Teeny Tiny Tino's Fishing Story* (Bordighera, 2008), was a winner of The 2008 Paterson Prize: Books for Young People Award. She self-published a collection of poems for young readers on topics her students asked for: *The Purple Potato and Other Poems*. Students with whom she has worked illustrated the poems in *The Purple Potato*.

Rachel's other books include her novel, *Tender Warriors*, and two other collections of poems, *How To Sing to a Dago*, and *Gambler's Daughter*.

She is past recipient of a New York Foundation Artist's Fellowship in fiction. She is poet-in-the-schools throughout central and upstate New York, and offers workshops independently. She lives in Cazenovia, NY.

VIA FOLIOS
A refereed book series dedicated to the culture of Italians and Italian Americans.

BERNARD J. BRUNO. *A Tear and A Tear in My Heart.* Vol 104 Fiction. $19
FELIX STEFANILE. *Songs of the Sparrow.* Vol 103 Poetry. $30
FRANK POLIZZI. *A New Life with Bianca.* Vol 102 Poetry. $12
GIL FAGIANI. *Stone Walls.* Vol 101 Poetry. $14
LOUISE DESALVO. *Casting Off.* Vol 100 Fiction. $22
MARY JO BONA. *I stop waiting for You.* Vol 99 Poetry. $12
RACHEL GUIDO DEVRIES. *Stati zitt, Josie.* Vol 98 Children's Literature. $8
GRACE CAVALIERI. *The Mandate of Heaven.* Vol 97 Poetry. $14
MARISA FRASCA. *Via incanto.* Vol 96 Poetry. $12
DOUGLAS GLADSTONE. *Carving a Niche for Himself.* Vol 95 History. $12
MARIA TERRONE. *Eye to Eye.* Vol 94 Poetry. $14
CONSTANCE SANCETTA. *Here in Cerchio* Vol 93 Local History. $15
MARIA MAZZIOTTI GILLAN. *Ancestors' Song* Vol 92 Poetry. $14
DARRELL FUSARO. *What if Godzilla Just Wanted a Hug?* Vol ? Essays. $TBA
MICHAEL PARENTI. *Waiting for Yesterday: Pages from a Street Kid's Life.* Vol 90 Memoir. $15
ANNIE LANZILOTTO, *Schistsong*, Vol. 89. Poetry, $15
EMANUEL DI PASQUALE, *Love Lines*, Vol. 88. Poetry, $10
CAROSONE & LOGIUDICE. *Our Naked Lives.* Vol 87 Essays. $15
JAMES PERICONI. *Strangers in a Strange Land: A Survey of Italian-Language American Books.* Vol. 86. Book History. $24
DANIELA GIOSEFFI, *Escaping La Vita Della Cucina*, Vol. 85. Essays & Creative Writing. $22
MARIA FAMÀ, *Mystics in the Family*, Vol. 84. Poetry, $10
ROSSANA DEL ZIO, *From Bread and Tomatoes to Zuppa di Pesce "Ciambotto"*, Vol. 83. $15
LORENZO DELBOCA, *Polentoni*, Vol. 82. Italian Studies, $15
SAMUEL GHELLI, *A Reference Grammar*, Vol. 81. Italian Language. $36
ROSS TALARICO, *Sled Run*, Vol. 80. Fiction. $15
FRED MISURELLA, *Only Sons*, Vol. 79. Fiction. $14
FRANK LENTRICCHIA, *The Portable Lentricchia*, Vol. 78. Fiction. $16
RICHARD VETERE, *The Other Colors in a Snow Storm*, Vol. 77. Poetry. $10
GARIBALDI LAPOLLA, *Fire in the Flesh*, Vol. 76 Fiction & Criticism. $25
GEORGE GUIDA, *The Pope Stories*, Vol. 75 Prose. $15
ROBERT VISCUSI, *Ellis Island*, Vol. 74. Poetry. $28
ELENA GIANINI BELOTTI, *The Bitter Taste of Strangers Bread*, Vol. 73, Fiction, $24
PINO APRILE, *Terroni*, Vol. 72, Italian Studies, $20
EMANUEL DI PASQUALE, *Harvest*, Vol. 71, Poetry, $10
ROBERT ZWEIG, *Return to Naples*, Vol. 70, Memoir, $16
AIROS & CAPPELLI, *Guido*, Vol. 69, Italian/American Studies, $12
FRED GARDAPHÉ, *Moustache Pete is Dead! Long Live Moustache Pete!*, Vol. 67, Literature/Oral History, $12
PAOLO RUFFILLI, *Dark Room/Camera oscura*, Vol. 66, Poetry, $11
HELEN BAROLINI, *Crossing the Alps*, Vol. 65, Fiction, $14
COSMO FERRARA, *Profiles of Italian Americans*, Vol. 64, Italian Americana, $16
GIL FAGIANI, *Chianti in Connecticut*, Vol. 63, Poetry, $10

Bordighera Press is an imprint of Bordighera, Incorporated, an independently owned not-for-profit scholarly organization that has no legal affiliation with the University of Central Florida or with The John D. Calandra Italian American Institute, Queens College/CUNY.

BASSETTI & D'ACQUINO, *Italic Lessons*, Vol. 62, Italian/American Studies, $10
CAVALIERI & PASCARELLI, Eds., *The Poet's Cookbook*, Vol. 61, Poetry/Recipes, $12
EMANUEL DI PASQUALE, *Siciliana*, Vol. 60, Poetry, $8
NATALIA COSTA, Ed., *Bufalini*, Vol. 59, Poetry. $18.
RICHARD VETERE, *Baroque*, Vol. 58, Fiction. $18.
LEWIS TURCO, *La Famiglia/The Family*, Vol. 57, Memoir, $15
NICK JAMES MILETI, *The Unscrupulous*, Vol. 56, Humanities, $20
BASSETTI, ACCOLLA, D'AQUINO, *Italici: An Encounter with Piero Bassetti*, Vol. 55, Italian Studies, $8
GIOSE RIMANELLI, *The Three-legged One*, Vol. 54, Fiction, $15
CHARLES KLOPP, *Bele Antiche Stòrie*, Vol. 53, Criticism, $25
JOSEPH RICAPITO, *Second Wave*, Vol. 52, Poetry, $12
GARY MORMINO, *Italians in Florida*, Vol. 51, History, $15
GIANFRANCO ANGELUCCI, *Federico F.*, Vol. 50, Fiction, $15
ANTHONY VALERIO, *The Little Sailor*, Vol. 49, Memoir, $9
ROSS TALARICO, *The Reptilian Interludes*, Vol. 48, Poetry, $15
RACHEL GUIDO DE VRIES, *Teeny Tiny Tino's Fishing Story*, Vol. 47, Children's Literature, $6
EMANUEL DI PASQUALE, *Writing Anew*, Vol. 46, Poetry, $15
MARIA FAMÀ, *Looking For Cover*, Vol. 45, Poetry, $12
ANTHONY VALERIO, *Toni Cade Bambara's One Sicilian Night*, Vol. 44, Poetry, $10
EMANUEL CARNEVALI, Dennis Barone, Ed., *Furnished Rooms*, Vol. 43, Poetry, $14
BRENT ADKINS, et al., Ed., *Shifting Borders, Negotiating Places*, Vol. 42, Proceedings, $18
GEORGE GUIDA, *Low Italian*, Vol. 41, Poetry, $11
GARDAPHÈ, GIORDANO, TAMBURRI, *Introducing Italian Americana*, Vol. 40, Italian/American Studies, $10
DANIELA GIOSEFFI, *Blood Autumn/Autunno di sangue*, Vol. 39, Poetry, $15/$25
FRED MISURELLA, *Lies to Live by*, Vol. 38, Stories, $15
STEVEN BELLUSCIO, *Constructing a Bibliography*, Vol. 37, Italian Americana, $15
ANTHONY JULIAN TAMBURRI, Ed., *Italian Cultural Studies 2002*, Vol. 36, Essays, $18
BEA TUSIANI, *con amore*, Vol. 35, Memoir, $19
FLAVIA BRIZIO-SKOV, Ed., *Reconstructing Societies in the Aftermath of War*, Vol. 34, History, $30
TAMBURRI, et al., Eds., *Italian Cultural Studies 2001*, Vol. 33, Essays, $18
ELIZABETH G. MESSINA, Ed., *In Our Own Voices*, Vol. 32, Italian/American Studies, $25
STANISLAO G. PUGLIESE, *Desperate Inscriptions*, Vol. 31, History, $12
HOSTERT & TAMBURRI, Eds., *Screening Ethnicity*, Vol. 30, Italian/American Culture, $25
G. PARATI & B. LAWTON, Eds., *Italian Cultural Studies*, Vol. 29, Essays, $18
HELEN BAROLINI, *More Italian Hours*, Vol. 28, Fiction, $16
FRANCO NASI, Ed., *Intorno alla Via Emilia*, Vol. 27, Culture, $16
ARTHUR L. CLEMENTS, *The Book of Madness & Love*, Vol. 26, Poetry, $10
JOHN CASEY, et al., *Imagining Humanity*, Vol. 25, Interdisciplinary Studies, $18
ROBERT LIMA, *Sardinia/Sardegna*, Vol. 24, Poetry, $10
DANIELA GIOSEFFI, *Going On*, Vol. 23, Poetry, $10
ROSS TALARICO, *The Journey Home*, Vol. 22, Poetry, $12
EMANUEL DI PASQUALE, *The Silver Lake Love Poems*, Vol. 21, Poetry, $7
JOSEPH TUSIANI, *Ethnicity*, Vol. 20, Poetry, $12
JENNIFER LAGIER, *Second Class Citizen*, Vol. 19, Poetry, $8
FELIX STEFANILE, *The Country of Absence*, Vol. 18, Poetry, $9
PHILIP CANNISTRARO, *Blackshirts*, Vol. 17, History, $12
LUIGI RUSTICHELLI, Ed., *Seminario sul racconto*, Vol. 16, Narrative, $10
LEWIS TURCO, *Shaking the Family Tree*, Vol. 15, Memoirs, $9

LUIGI RUSTICHELLI, Ed., *Seminario sulla drammaturgia*, Vol. 14, Theater/Essays, $10

FRED GARDAPHÈ, *Moustache Pete is Dead! Long Live Moustache Pete!*, Vol. 13, Oral Literature, $10

JONE GAILLARD CORSI, *Il libretto d'autore*, 1860–1930, Vol. 12, Criticism, $17

HELEN BAROLINI, *Chiaroscuro: Essays of Identity*, Vol. 11, Essays, $15

PICARAZZI & FEINSTEIN, Eds., *An African Harlequin in Milan*, Vol. 10, Theater/Essays, $15

JOSEPH RICAPITO, *Florentine Streets & Other Poems*, Vol. 9, Poetry, $9

FRED MISURELLA, *Short Time*, Vol. 8, Novella, $7

NED CONDINI, *Quartettsatz*, Vol. 7, Poetry, $7

ANTHONY JULIAN TAMBURRI, Ed., *Fuori: Essays by Italian/American Lesbians and Gays*, Vol. 6, Essays, $10

ANTONIO GRAMSCI, P. Verdicchio, Trans. & Intro., *The Southern Question*, Vol. 5, Social Criticism, $5

DANIELA GIOSEFFI, *Word Wounds & Water Flowers*, Vol. 4, Poetry, $8

WILEY FEINSTEIN, *Humility's Deceit: Calvino Reading Ariosto Reading Calvino*, Vol. 3, Criticism, $10

PAOLO A. GIORDANO, Ed., *Joseph Tusiani: Poet, Translator, Humanist*, Vol. 2, Criticism, $25

ROBERT VISCUSI, *Oration Upon the Most Recent Death of Christopher Columbus*, Vol. 1, Poetry, $3

www.ingramcontent.com/pod-product-compliance
Lightning Source LLC
Chambersburg PA
CBHW020020050426
42450CB00005B/568